WRAPPED IN WHIRLWINDS

Poems of The Crimean War

WRAPPED IN WHIRLWINDS

Poems of The Crimean War

by

Harry Turner

SPELLMOUNT
Staplehurst

British Library Cataloguing in Publication Data:

A catalogue record for this book is available
from the British Library

Copyright © Harry Turner 2005
Maps copyright © Spellmount Ltd 2005

ISBN 1-86227-279-4

First published in the UK in 2005 by
Spellmount Limited
The Village Centre
Staplehurst
Kent TN12 OBJ

Tel: 01580 893730
Fax: 01580 893731
E-mail: enquiries@spellmount.com
Website: www.spellmount.com

1 3 5 7 9 8 6 4 2

Typeset in Palatino by MATS, Southend-on-Sea, Essex
Printed in Great Britain by
Oaklands Book Services
Stonehouse, Gloucester GL10 3RQ

Contents

This book is dedicated to the
ordinary soldiers, infantrymen,
cavalrymen, gunners, sappers
and medical orderlies of Britain,
Russia, Turkey and France.

Author's Note

I am grateful to the following sources which afforded me much inspiration when writing this book.

Adkin, Mark, *The Charge*, Leo Cooper, 1996
David, Saul, *The Homicidal Earl*, Little, Brown, 1997
Fletcher, Ian and Ishchenko, Natalia, *The Crimean War.
    A Clash of Empires*, Spellmount, 2004
Hibbert, Christopher, *The Destruction of Lord Raglan*,
    Longman, 1961
Mercer, Patrick, *'Give Them a Volley and Charge!'. The Battle of
    Inkerman, 1854*, Spellmount, 1998
Mercer, Patrick, *Inkerman 1854*, Osprey, 1998
Morris, Jan, *Pax Britannica*, Vols 1–3, Faber & Faber, 1968
Royle, Trevor, *Crimea*, Little, Brown, 1999
Sweetman, John, *The Crimean War*, Osprey, 2001
Tolstoy, Leo, *The Raid*, Oxford University Press, 1906
Tyrell, Henry, *War with Russia*, Vols 1–3, London Printing,
    1895
Warner, Philip, *Letters from the Crimea*, John Murray, 1977
Woodham-Smith, Cecil, *The Reason Why*, Constable, 1953

I am also indebted to Patrick Mercer MP and Ian Fletcher, two formidable military historians, who helped fan my enthusiasm for this, the last in my trilogy of heroes. It was Patrick who led me on my first Charge of the Light Brigade in the Valley of Death, during a spectacular Ukrainian thunderstorm; also my colleague from the 57th Regiment ('The Diehards'), John Talbot, who lent me his three ancient volumes of Henry Tyrell's *War with Russia*.

I must thank Larissa Kazachenko of the Crimean Tourist Association and Dr Natalia Ishchenko, Assistant Professor of the Crimean Research Centre in the Ukraine, who illuminated my first visit to the Crimea with their knowledge, enthusiasm and charm. Also the splendid staff at the National Army Museum, Apsley House, Windsor Castle and the British Museum, all of which are treasure houses of British history.

Foreword

The British Army that landed on the shores of the Crimea was a mere shadow of the great force that fought under Wellington in the Peninsular War. Its generals were by and large old men with little battle experience, and although they won through in the end, it was a conflict punctuated by administrative bungling, inadequate supplies and the scourge of cholera, a disease that killed more men than enemy guns.

The British Commander, Lord Raglan, a courtly and decent gentleman, was a protégé of the Duke of Wellington and had lost an arm at the Battle of Waterloo, but he was in no way fit to stand in Wellington's boots.

When, in 1783, Catherine the Great of Russia annexed the Crimea, her actions triggered a series of adventures in and around the Black Sea that led, piece-by-piece, to Russia finally invading Moldavia and Wallachia in 1853. In October that year, 'little' Turkey declared war on mighty Russia and Turkey's ally, Britain, was drawn into the quarrel. But we also feared that Russia's expansion plans might threaten our trade routes to India. Britain therefore demanded Russia's withdrawal from Moldavia and Wallachia, which surprise, surprise, they refused to do. By the end of March, both Britain and France had declared war on Russia.

France, our ancient enemy, was now our friend, even though Lord Raglan had to be constantly reminded of the fact by his aides.

Hoping for a speedy *coup de main*, the allies had landed in the Crimea and fought their way towards Sevastopol. With the Russian fleet trapped in its own Black Sea port, the Anglo–French command felt it would be a simple matter to seize their great quarry, Sevastopol, with little difficulty.

In the event, it was a stumbling, bloody affair. Apart from

disease, the supply chain was woefully inadequate, adding to the hardships and difficulties facing our soldiers.

Sevastopol was stoutly defended and absorbed staggering bombardments from French and English guns. Some battles were futile and, although the common soldiers on both sides acquitted themselves nobly, good generalship was often lacking.

The Crimean War spawned many stories, often exaggerated, about individual battles. Most schoolboys know of the famous Charge of The Light Brigade, but there were other equally bloody clashes, and at the end of the conflict, both sides wondered whether they should have gone to war in the first place

It is ironic, contemplating those events now in 2005, to realise that we went to war to protect a corrupt Islamic state, Turkey, the sick man of Europe, against the mighty Russian nation whose Czar was a blood relative of our own Queen Victoria.

This book reflects on the events of this great conflict that took place on the wide borders twixt Europe and the mighty continent of Asia. It mirrors the heroism of the common soldiers on both sides and the weaknesses of some of the senior generals. It touches on the dreadful sickness that struck down so many men, and briefly records the role that the famous nurse, Florence Nightingale, played in the affair. It also records the gigantic loss of life that resulted from the ferocious sieges at Sevastopol and the conditions under which both the besieged and the besiegers fought in their deadly struggle.

It also illustrates the inadequacy of the administrative arrangements, the lack of supplies, the appalling field hospitals and the mendacity of some of the politicians back at home – a sad feature of all war stories whether ancient or modern.

I have chosen to re-tell the story of the Crimea in verse because I thought it would be an appropriate way to carry the narrative forward and recapture some of the drama and excitement of that extraordinary period of British history, a period that the Czar of Russia once described as like being 'Wrapped in Whirlwinds'.

Harry Turner
Deepcut, 2005

The Poems

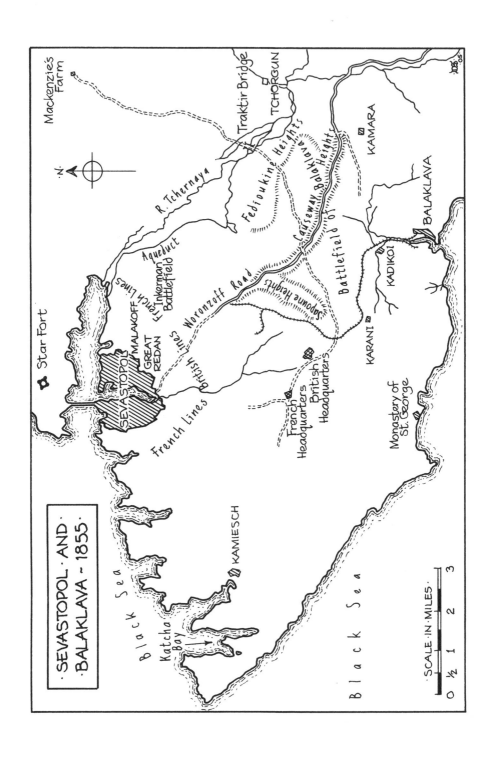

· SEVASTOPOL · AND ·
· BALAKLAVA ~ 1855 ·

Mackenzie's Farm

Traktir Bridge

TCHORGUN

Fedioukine Heights

KAMARA

Balaclava Heights

Causeway

R. Tchernaya

Battlefield of

BALAKLAVA

·N·

Star Fort

Aqueduct

French Lines

Inkerman Battlefield

MALAKOFF

KADIKOI

KARANI

Woronzoff Road

Sapoune Heights

British Lines

SEVASTOPOL

GREAT REDAN

French Lines

British Headquarters

French Headquarters

Monastery of St. George

Black Sea

KAMIESCH

Katcha Bay

Black Sea

Black Sea

· SCALE · IN · MILES ·

0   ½   1   2   3

1

THE PROLOGUE –
NOVEMBER 1853

See the Czar of all the Russias,
Clad in silk and draped in sable,
In his gilded, mirrored palace,
At his gold-topped writing table.

See the objects there before him,
Parchment sheets and feathered pen,
Surrounded by his loyal courtiers,
Bearded Cossacks, holy men.

'Let Te Deum be sung in churches'
Is the Czar's triumphant cry.
Celebrate a Russian victory,
Praise our warriors to the sky.

For Nachimoff, the Russian admiral
Has thrown his squadron 'gainst the Turk.
All their ships are sunk or shattered,
A fearsome, brutal piece of work.

Lying in Sinope harbour,
Ill-prepared for such a fight,
Turks are slaughtered in their thousands,
Crushed like ants by Russian might.

Plunging to the ocean's bottom,
Canvas, timbers, guns and ropes,
The Turkish fleet is quite destroyed now,
And with it little Turkey's hopes.

Now we see Britannia stirring,
Talk of war is in the air.
Should Victoria aid poor Turkey?
Sanction war against the Bear?

Men and horses, guns and rations
Are loaded onto British ships.
Soon to sail and challenge Russia,
All are keen to get to grips.

By early spring fierce fighting's started,
French and English side by side.
But the drama that's unfolding
Ebbs and flows like summer tide.

None can see or even guess at
How this contretemps will end,
How much blood and how much treasure
Will be shed for wounds to mend.

How decades will pass like shadows
Casting shapes across the years,
How the scribes will fill up volumes,
History drenched in widows' tears.

Was it worth it? Or just futile?
Was it noble? Wrong or right?
Did we really have to be there?
Was it all a pointless fight?

There are answers to these questions,
But they differ one from one.
Argument will still continue
From daylight to the setting sun.

One thing constant does emerge though,
Shining through the mists of time.
Common soldiers in their thousands
All showed courage quite sublime.

Raise your glass then and salute them,
As you study history's works,
The toast is 'All the common soldiers,
British, Frenchmen, Russians, Turks'.

2

THE LAST QUADRILLE

The swirl of silk, the gleam of pearls
Beneath the chandeliers,
A brisk quadrille like army drill
Can't mask emerging fears.

The soaring strains of violins,
The clink of champagne glasses.
As over old Lord Raglan's brow
A cloud of worry passes.

He hears a distant drumbeat,
And a muffled bugle call,
But only he perceives it
Inside that painted hall.

He knows a war is looming,
And the nation's blood is up,
Thus very soon he'll take a drink
From conflict's bitter cup.

His phantom arm is aching,
'Tis decades since last he fought,
Are Wellington's words remembered?
Can he recall what he was taught?

For close to fifty years have passed
Since the field of Waterloo.
Before that fight, on such a night
They danced a quadrille too.

The ghosts of men who fought back then
Now painful to recall,
Flit silently inside his head
Like shadows at the ball.

'Tis Turkey – little Turkey
Who is victim of the bear.
The mighty paw of Russia's poised
To crush and rend and tear.

So Britain must defend her,
Spend men and blood and treasure,
Beside unlikely ally France
To get the Czar's full measure.

More images fill Raglan's mind,
Of foam-flecked horses prancing,
And gaping wounds like open mouths,
While before him there's still dancing –

By subalterns, like frisky colts
In uniforms resplendent,
And on such youths all pep and dash
Will Raglan be dependent.

The die is cast, no turning back,
His duty is quite plain,
He'll serve Victoria his Queen
Through hazards, grief and pain.

This decent, muddled gentleman,
This old Horse-Guards grandee,
Is just a man whom fate has touched,
No warrior is he.

Tomorrow he'll be sailing,
As sunrise paints the dawn,
And from the arms of loved ones,
Many young men will be torn.

But now the ball is ended
By the candles' flickering glow
In the sconces on the panelling,
Casting shadows soft and low.

Raglan hears a distant drumbeat,
And a muffled bugle call,
But only he perceives it
In that empty, painted hall.

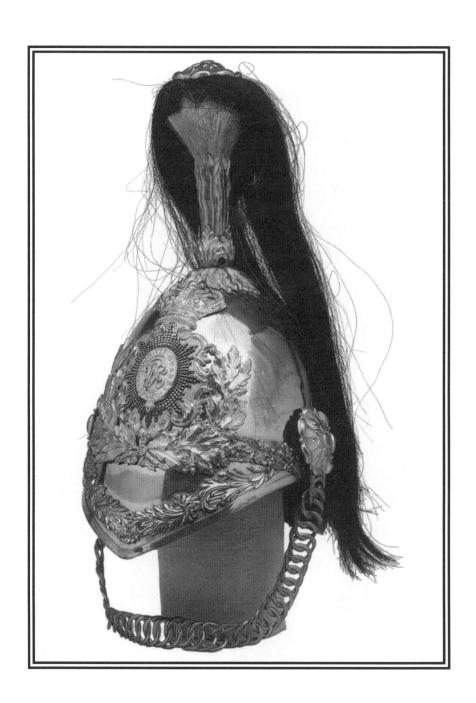

3
A MAGNIFICENT SPECTACLE

From a cloudless sky of azure blue
Came shafts of sunlight streaming.
On sixty thousand marching men,
Each lance and helmet gleaming.

Epaulettes, buttons, pouches and brass,
Cross-belts of dazzling white,
Gold-laced pelisses and fluttering plumes,
Black shakos reflecting the light.

Each regiment's colours unfurled now,
Silk squares that dance in the breeze,
Scarlet and yellow and golden and black,
Like a forest of rainbow-kissed trees.

Guardsmen, Hussars and Artillery,
In tunics of blood red and green,
Blazing, magnificent, awesome and proud,
A heart-stopping, breath-catching scene.

But proudest perhaps, were the Horsemen
On their mounts with their shimmering coats.
And no man could know just how far they must go
Till those beasts could again feast on oats.

And the bands played with confident brio,
Sounding bugles alongside the drummers,
Famous tunes to send British hearts leaping,
Which appealed to all ranks and all comers.

The jingle of harness, of scabbards, of spurs,
The soft slap of leather so pliant,
And the tall Guardsmen's bearskins towering high
Making each gallant soldier a giant.

To the right of our line were the Frenchmen,
Marching close to the sea and the fleet.
While farther inland was Lord Raglan,
His appearance most sombre and neat.

In two mighty columns the armies now marched,
Over wild thyme and soft springy turf,
And mixed with the sounds of the military bands
Came the faint hiss of far distant surf.

This then was a glorious moment,
A prelude to what was to come,
As with lengthening stride and hearts filled with pride,
And their bayonets lit by the sun.

But deep in the ranks of this carnival,
This portrait of dash and of pluck,
Lurked a horror much worse than the enemy,
As the nightmare of cholera struck.

But men will recall with affection,
When the tales of old battles are told,
Of the march of the army that morning,
That first sight so stirring and bold.

Years pass and still we remember,
With sadness and wonder and pride,
The feats and the acts of raw courage,
By our soldiers who fought there and died.

4

THE EVE OF ALMA

Salt pork and biscuit, a cupful of rum,
An' a pipe of damp baccy to follow.
This luxury feast is the most, not the least
In which a poor fellow can wallow.

Out here on the plain it's all cold wind and rain,
An' we 'aint got no tents to protect us.
The lads are all plucky, and for me, well I'm lucky
'Cos so far that foul plague* don't affect us.

But me feet are swollen and puffy,
And me teeth have grown loose in me head,
An' I've shat in me breeches and that rots the stitches,
But praise God, Mum, I'm breathing, not dead.

We're 'ere to fight Russia, or is it just Prussia?
I'm beggared to know why we're here,
'Cos instead of the rum and the sound of the drum,
I'd like to be home, drinking beer.

Tomorrow at dawn when we're mustered,
We'll put on our shakos and packs,
With rifles and bullets and tunics,
That's a forty pound weight on each back.

Something big is afoot, says our sergeant,
And we'll meet with those Russkies at last,
At a place on the map I 'aint seen yet,
Where a river called 'Alma' flows fast.

* Cholera

I must stop now and finish this letter,
And 'ope that it reaches you soon,
As the campfire is flickering dimly
And there's no light from the watery moon.

I pray when you do get my letter,
The fightin' and killin' is done,
Don't want to distress you dear Mum and God bless you,
Goodnight now from your loving son.

5

THE ROAD TO THE ALMA

You can smell an army from afar
By the reek of dung and leather,
And the equine tang of horse's sweat
Mixed with the scent of heather.

On Chobham Common's springy turf;
Unscarred by rock or boulder,
Lord Cardigan's pink-trousered men
Sit shoulder next to shoulder.

Each man is neat, from head to feet,
Each sword blade glittering bright,
Each saddle burnished to a shine,
Each uniform skin-tight.

The Sergeants on black horses
That arch their necks and prance,
And hard-faced men within the ranks,
Each holding high a lance.

And at their head the colours fly
In the gentle Surrey breeze,
The horses snort and stamp and neigh,
Some others simply sneeze.

At last the order's given,
They will advance in line.
And men and beasts are grateful
For this long awaited sign.

They walk, they trot, they canter,
They manoeuvre to and fro.
Their movements are like clockwork
In this fine equestrian show.

But such displays of horsemanship,
All vanity and dash,
Is preparation for a bitter truth,
Sharp as a sabre slash.

For soon these men and horses
Will face a bloody battle,
Where uniforms will hang in shreds,
'Gainst blades their own will rattle.

And mixed with the smell of leather,
And dung, and churned up mud,
They'll no longer be smelling the heather,
But the acrid stench of blood.

Others who manoeuvred at Chobham
Under England's unthreatening sky,
Were unschooled in the dark arts of warfare,
Couldn't conceive that they might die.

'Twas a game and a laugh and a gamble,
A change from dull barracks routine,
Where the air was as clear as a glass of cold beer,
And the grass was an emerald green.

Thus a few weeks of training at Chobham,
Even three weeks, a month or much more,
Was never a full preparation
For the blistering horror of war.

For the journey to war was a nightmare,
A hazardous voyage by sea.
They saw lives lost, by storms they were tossed,
Fearful now what their future might be.

When the ships arrived safe at the harbour,
Men were sick with the fever or dead,
And the corpses of horses were dropped overboard,
Turning foamy-tipped waves bloody red.

The beach was a scene of confusion,
As the ships prepared to unload,
All the paraphernalia of soldiers,
Being carried or dragged to the road.

Guns and baskets and limbers, some with half shattered timbers,
Army biscuits and bullets and tack.
There were casks full of rum for the soldiers,
And horse feed packed loose in each sack.

There were boxes and chests by the dozen,
And wagons with huge wooden wheels,
And shovels with handles, and baccy and candles,
And dried mutton for poor wretches' meals.

Through the waves and the sand and the garbage,
Soldiers waded waist-high in the spume,
Some collapsed with the fever unheeded,
Adding pathos to gathering gloom.

Men struggled all day in Calamita Bay,
In a welter of chaos and muddle.
The logistical plan was a hideous sham,
As soldiers crouched round in a huddle.

Commissary men on the shoreline,
Were forced to decide on the spot,
Which supplies would be dumped on the beaches,
And which others, more vital, would not.

Midst the stench and the bustle, they struggled in vain,
As more soldiers splashed in from the boats,
And waves curled ashore with a splattering roar,
Drenching wet several sacks of dry oats.

The clouds high above turned to purple,
And dead horses swelled up in the foam,
As swarms of black flies now darkened the skies,
And boy soldiers wished they'd stayed home.

In order, shambolic, many men sick with colic,
They finally mustered ashore,
Urged by bugle and drum, they manhandled each gun
With their colours well up to the fore.

Thus at last came the march to the Alma,
A river fast-flowing and deep.
Men were ragged and hungry and frightened,
And exhausted from too little sleep.

On the slopes just ahead were the Russians,
A daunting formidable sight,
Artillery, lancers and Cossacks,
Eight thousand – just waiting to fight.

But Lord Raglan was not to be temped,
Discretion – not valour – his vow.
Why risk an attack, he could even draw back,
Keep his cavalry 'band-boxed'* for now.

Four squadrons were told to stand steady,
No mad provocation allowed,
No dash, no heroics, all men to be stoics,
Was the order passed down clear and loud.

The Russians amazed at this tactic,
Had expected a massive attack,
So they jeered and they cheered as to them it appeared,
The British were skulking right back.

British cavalrymen all were frustrated,
Lord Lucan, their General, was blamed,
They dubbed him Lord 'Look-On' in anger,
They felt comprehensively shamed.

* Lord Raglan was very protective towards his precious cavalry and
preferred to utilise them very sparingly, keeping them, it was said
metaphorically, 'in a bandbox'.

Thus the battle began the morning,
Specific to Raglan's request,
And on the far side of the river,
The Russians were facing a test.

Prince Menshikov, who was commanding,
Had established a position of strength,
With his men on the slopes of the Kourgane,
With redoubts along most of its length.

But these earthworks and fortifications,
Constructed to house Russian guns,
Failed to quell the advance of the British,
And the Czar's army lost many fine sons.

The fight was ferocious, the killing atrocious,
No quarter was given or taken,
With hundreds expiring from the fierce British firing,
Many Russians felt they'd been forsaken.

The front line had wavered, bitter death they had savoured,
And now they fell back in retreat,
With British advancing, bright colours still dancing,
With the riverbank now at their feet.

In the Alma they plunged, bayonets gleaming,
And up the steep slope right ahead,
With a full-throated shout, they scaled the redoubt,
Treading hard over poor Russian dead.

Prince Menshikov now faced disaster,
He turned to a comrade and cried,
'This is a disgrace to the proud Russian race,
T'would be better if all of us died.'

It was all much too late to reverse this sad fate,
As the Redcoats swarmed over the hill,
And Menshikov knew they'd been scattered,
Like pheasants driven out for the kill.

The taste of victory is sweet,
But the price is rank and bitter,
As men with broken, blooded limbs,
Sprawl on the hill like litter.

But triumph is the epilogue,
Of this most famous victory,
As French and British soldiers' names
Are immortalised in history.

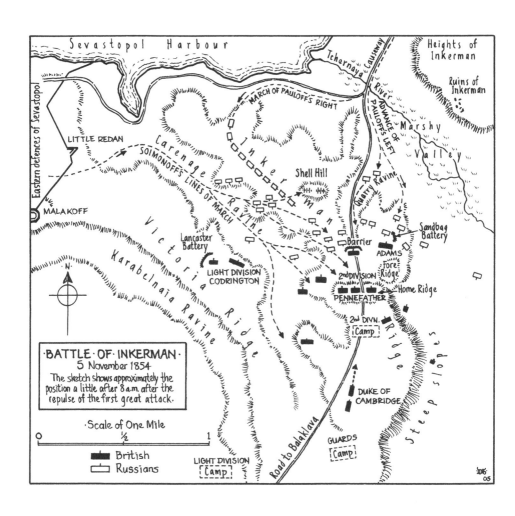

Sevastopol   Harbour

Heights of
Inkerman

Tchernaya

Causeway

River

Ruins of
Inkerman

MARCH OF PAULOFF'S RIGHT

ADVANCE OF PAULOFF'S LEFT

Marshy

LITTLE REDAN

Carenage

SOIMONOFF'S LINES OF MARCH

Eastern defences of Sevastopol

Valley

Shell Hill

Quarry Ravine

MALAKOFF

Sandbag
Battery

Ravine

Inkerman

Lancaster
Battery

Barrier

ADAMS

Victoria

LIGHT DIVISION
CODRINGTON

2ᵈ DIVISION

fore
Ridge

Home Ridge

N

Karabelnaia

Ridge

PENNEFATHER

Ridge

Ravine

Steep slopes

2ⁿᵈ DIVN.
Camp

·BATTLE·OF·INKERMAN·
5 November 1854
The sketch shows approximately the
position a little after 8 a.m. after the
repulse of the first great attack.

DUKE OF
CAMBRIDGE

·Scale of One Mile·
0   ½   1

GUARDS
Camp

British
Russians

LIGHT DIVISION
Camp

Road to Balaklava

bms
05

6

PARASOLS AND BONNETS

With gaily coloured parasols
And flowers in their bonnets,
They scaled the heights like dainty sprites,
Some singing words from sonnets.

They set their picnic tables down,
Laid neat with glass and china,
On lacy cloths of purest white,
Crowned kings could boast none finer.

These ladies in their smartest clothes,
Grey shoes and Paris gloves,
Ate cake and fruit and sipped hot tea
As innocent as doves.

But they were there to witness death
Below them on the plain,
To cheer or faint as sweating men
Inflicted wounds and pain.

Both sides, alas, contributed
To this audience most ghoulish,
And very few refused to view
From fear of looking foolish.

At the battle of the Alma though,
That hard won, bloody fight,
Prince Menshikov's invited guests
Were forced to sudden flight.

Behind them scattered on the hill,
Were parasols and bonnets,
One shouldn't gloat, but merely note,
They were no longer singing sonnets.

7

SCUTARI

In wretched rows like gutted fish,
Deep sabre cuts still bleeding,
No soap, no towels, no bandages,
So few to hear their pleading.

Each wounded soldier racked with pain,
On a stinking lice-filled bed,
A charnel house come hot from hell,
A vortex for the dead.

The severed limbs, the gaping wounds,
The groans and whispered prayers,
The stoics and hysterics,
The dying men's cold stares.

The floors awash with filth and gore,
The roof tiles cracked and leaking,
And through the crumbling window frames,
A fearsome wind comes shrieking.

Companion to the wounds of war
Comes a plague of foul diseases,
Hobgoblins bearing cholera
On silent lethal breezes.

Ten thousand dead? Nay, maybe more
Before this war was ended.
For pity's sake was this the thing
That England had intended?

Meantime back home, the news arrives,
A shocking revelation,
That fires the blood and fiercely pricks
The conscience of the nation.

This news is published in *The Times*,
And read by swells and fops.
It's read aloud by ladies too
In Mayfair coffee shops.

And errand boys and dowagers,
And coachmen, grooms and tailors,
Demanding 'something must be done
For our soldiers and our sailors'.

But a nation's rage and pain alone
Is nought but empty sound.
What's needed now's a catalyst
To turn the crisis round.

In London's famous Harley Street,
Sits one who sheds few tears,
A stern Victorian lady,
Mature beyond her years.

A product of the moneyed class,
Self-righteous, shrill and terse,
With the steely dedication found
In a bourgeois English nurse.

She reads *The Times* with furrowed brow,
Aghast and deeply shaken,
Her sense of moral outrage stirred
For her kinsmen so forsaken.

She sits alone by candlelight,
And pens a vital letter
To the Secretary of War no less,
For contacts come no better.

'I am the one,' she boldly states,
'To organise a scheme,
Recruiting groups of nurses *now*,
I'll be leader of the team.'

'I'll train them and I'll rule them
And I'll take them to the war,
And I'll set up proper hospitals –
I'll do this and much, much more.'

And so she did, and did it well,
In those wretched Crimea camps,
And thus began the legend of
The ladies with the lamps.

Be under no illusion though,
Dear Florence was no saint,
Efficient, tough, resourceful
And as hard as fresh-dried paint.

Let's remember her with gratitude,
As we raise our glass of wine.
Florence Nightingale we salute you,
English lady – most sublime.

8

THE BASHI-BAZOUKS

Through veils of dust and shimmering heat,
Beneath the sun's cruel hammer,
On the scorched anvil of the earth,
They rode midst noise and clamour.

A motley crew of cut-throat rogues,
Ferocious to behold,
Cast by their God, most carelessly
From a long-since broken mould.

They were Eastern Condottieri, *
Big, shaggy-bearded brutes,
All kinsmen of old Saladin
With ancient savage roots.

Their faces lined and fissured
Through exposure to the weather,
Eyes bright like hawks' in search of prey,
Skins tanned like saddle leather.

These were the vulpine vagabonds
The British hoped to tame.
But discipline to such wild men
Was nothing but a game.

---

* Irregulars of mixed race, Turkish, Nubian, Arab, Albanian. They fought
under Omar Pasha in the 1853 Danubian campaign. Later when under
the command in the Crimea of Major-General Beatson, they became
known jokingly as 'Beatson's Horse'. Later commanded by Brigadier
Brett and Major-General Smith, they were never called to action. Most
historians agree, had they been allowed to fight, they would have been
formidable.

Right through the allied lines they rode,
Past British, Turks and French,
And from their ranks and heaving flanks
Arose a fearful stench.

They bivouacked near Varna,
Lit fires and smoked their pipes,
Erected tents of animal hides,
Ate bowls of rancid tripes.

They piled their ancient weapons up,
Huge sabres, muskets, pikes.
Some wore strange helmets chased in brass
With fearsome pointed spikes.

You couldn't ever wish to see
Scoundrels more picturesque.
Lord Raglan was apprised of this
As he sat behind his desk.

His tent was hot and so was he,
Wind had blown in from hell,
And though a mile from the Bashi camp,
He could still detect their smell.

'These fellows are uncivilised,'
Lord Raglan now complained.
'They're villains and Barbarians,
We'll never get them trained.

'I've heard the most unsettling tales
Of arson, rape and plunder,
How they chop off the Bulgar's hands,
And rip young girls asunder.'

But nonetheless, in spite of this
And other fierce discussions,
The Bashis soon were saddled up
To help us fight the Russians.

Alas however, history shows
That argument pernicious,
Among the allied high command
Became tortuous and vicious.

We found it hard to comprehend
How the swirling Bashi ranks
Would not respond to discipline,
Preferring madcap pranks.

Thus it was these fighting men,
These warriors wild and strong,
Were never actually called to fight
Or sing their battle song.

Is it fruitless now to speculate
What might have happened then,
If the Bashis had stood side-by-side
With British fighting men.

So toss a coin, gaze in a glass,
Conjure a different ending.
Imagine how it could have been
With the Bashi hordes descending.

On Inkerman, Sevastopol,
Even Alma and some others,
With those hairy, bloodstained, crazy men,
Alongside us as our brothers!

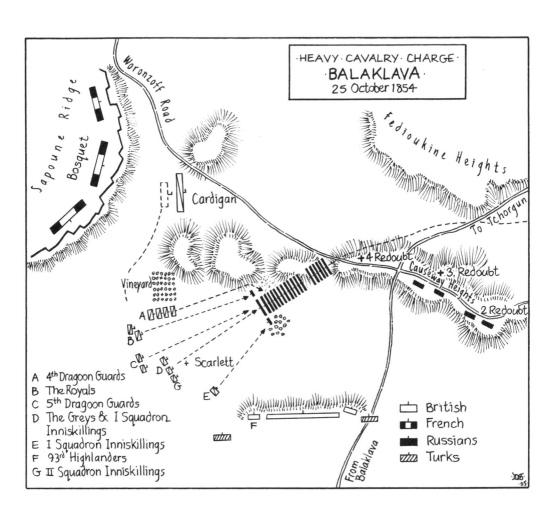

Sapoune Ridge

Bosquet

Woronzoff Road

Fedioukine Heights

To Tchorgun

Cardigan

+ 4 Redoubt

Causeway Heights

+ 3. Redoubt

Vineyard

2 Redoubt

A

B

C

D

G

+ Scarlett

E

F

A 4th Dragoon Guards
B The Royals
C 5th Dragoon Guards
D The Greys & I Squadron
    Inniskillings
E I Squadron Inniskillings
F 93rd Highlanders
G II Squadron Inniskillings

From Balaklava

British
French
Russians
Turks

9

THE CHARGE
OF THE HEAVY BRIGADE

Beyond the Causeway Heights they sat
As their chargers pawed the turf;
Each man resolved to live or die,
And prove his soldier's worth.

They were the men of the Heavy Brigade,
*General Scarlett there, commanding.
Each trooper knew he faced a task,
Both dangerous and demanding.

The man from *The Times*** in attendance,
Heard the clink of the sabres below,
And the jingle of bits, as the horses
Were lined up and dressed, row by row.

Unsupported but moving like chessmen,
The Heavy Brigade would advance,
Til ahead on the slopes of the causeway,
They observed forests of bright Russian lance.

With his 'Indian'*** Officers round him,
General Scarlett prepared to attack,
Taking ground to the right, he manoeuvred
Scots Greys and Dragoons at his back.

---

* Sir James Scarlett 1799–1871, Eton & Cambridge, Conservative MP for
Guildford 1836–1841, Commanding the Heavy Brigade.
** William Howard Russell, *The Times* War Correspondent.
*** Officers who had served in India were often regarded as being
somewhat inferior. Cardigan himself took a snobbish and disdainful
view of them, a quite ridiculous attitude when you consider that the
greatest British soldier of all time, Wellington, once served in India in the
early part of his career.

The Russians observed this scene calmly,
As they crested the ridge just ahead.
They were three thousand strong on fine horses,
Sitting motionless, waiting 'tis said.

In enormously thick, heavy topcoats,
Helmets glinting like gold in the sun,
The Russians presented a phalanx,
A challenge to be overcome.

Scarlett's 'Heavies' were less than six hundred,
Resplendent in tunics of red,
Looking frail though, compared to the Russians
Who were massed on the slope just ahead.

At length General Scarlett was settled,
His cavalry lined up and smart.
Their drill was straight from the text book,
Horses pawing, impatient to start.

Beside him rode ADC Elliott,
A Lieutenant of 'Indian' fame,
Who under instruction from Scarlett,
Was properly dressed for the game.

His cocked hat was loose and ill-fitting,
But aware of old Scarlett's decree,
A handkerchief now filled the gap,
Of pure silk for comrades to see.

Red-faced now, and eager, the General
Turned right in his saddle and cried,
'Sound the charge' as he withdrew his sabre,
Moving forward with men at each side.

'Come on lads,' cried Scarlett exultant,
As he galloped straight into the fray,
Where the motionless Russians observed him
With a mixture of awe and dismay.

As his charger came thundering forward,
A Russian stood flanking his way,
But he drove his horse faster, avoiding disaster,
Determined to triumph this day.

Behind him with sabre extended
Was Elliott, fired-up and keen,
Who skewered the Russian completely,
Piercing clean through the poor fellow's spleen.

Then the pale-faced Lieutenant and Scarlett,
Swallowed up by the massed Russian troops,
Were hacking and cutting and stabbing,
Scarlett letting out full-throated whoops.

So closely packed in were the soldiers,
As the heavies moved up to engage,
That no skill of the sword was on offer,
Just brute strength fuelled by blood, lust and rage.

The Scots Greys and the brave Iniskillings,
Were now in the midst of the ruck,
And Scarlett himself took five stab wounds,
And Elliott, too, had bad luck.

His cocked-hat was just like a magnet,
A target for sabre and lance,
He took fourteen fierce cuts to the body,
As his terrified horse shied and pranced.

Unconscious, he slumped in his saddle
As a sabre blade slashed through the air,
It cleaved through his hat just like butter,
But the square of fine silk was still there.

It had shielded his skull from the sabre,
As his horse pulled away from the fight,
But around him the battle continued,
Swords and lances, with blood, shining bright.

The Russians were clad in their topcoats
Of a cloth both unyielding and thick,
So the cuts from the sabres just bounced off
Unless wielded to stab or to stick.

'Twas eight minutes since Scarlett had started,
With the fighting ground churned up and muddy,
Hacking and swearing and sweating like pigs,
Both sides were now filthy and bloody.

A few men from the Light now joined in the fight,
Mixed in with the struggling hordes,
Two butchers, both brothers, along with the others
Were wielding meat-cleavers like swords.

And then in an instant the Russians pulled back,
Bruised, battered, demoralised, ragged,
Retreating now in broken ranks,
Their lines unkempt and jagged.

Right over the Woronzoff Road they fled,
On up to the Causeway Heights.
The British watchers on the hillside cheered,
'Twas a glorious, stirring sight.

The Commander-in-Chief, old Lord Raglan,
So pleased with the Heavies' success,
Sent an ADC down to see Scarlett,
He could hardly do anything less.

'Well done,' said the note in Raglan's hand,
For the victory was quick and quite splendid,
And Scarlett turned, so they'd not see his tears,
As his most gallant dash had now ended.

But sitting nearby just observing,
Lord Cardigan, less than ecstatic,
'They have the laugh on us,' cried he,
In a voice that was gruff and dramatic.

'Damn those Heavies!' he said, moustache bristling,
For they'd showed up his dear Light Brigade,
To add insult to pain, his cries were in vain,
As for action he fervently prayed.

But no orders had come from Lord Lucan,
For his 'Cherry Bums'* now to move out,
As a flanking attack, as the Russians drew back,
Would have turned victory into a rout.

And thus on this day on those hillsides,
The Heavy Brigade were supreme,
But the passage of time is corrosive,
Making many assume 'twas a dream.

Somewhat later that day in the valley,
The Light Brigade's honour revived,
Restoring their great reputation,
Making heroes of those who had survived.

---

* Cardigan's men were nicknamed the 'Cherry Bums' because of their
cherry coloured, tight cavalry pants.

10

THE OBSERVER

Under the empty cobalt sky,
By sheaves of trembling corn,
He sees each detail vividly,
All images new born.

Sweet to his eye, miraculous,
The trees, the grass, the plain,
The butterflies and blue-black crows,
And the smell of distant rain.

The sound of drums still muffled,
The shrill note of a pipe,
The tramp of feet, so bittersweet,
For his memory is ripe.

The horses and the donkeys,
Some draped in sheepskin coats,
The gleam of shiny leather,
The sweet smell of fresh oats.

The observer sees most everything,
It's locked in his fertile brain,
As Chechens and Ukrainians
Trudge o'er the yawning plain.

Line upon line of marching men,
With pipes and water flasks,
And sabres curved like devil's horns,
And dark brown powder casks.

Some men are bearded like the 'pard'*,
Backs doubled with fatigue,
And there's a priest in bible-black
Who's limped for half a league.

The crucifix around his throat
He fingers as he prays.
His feet are numb, and he'll succumb
His lifespan in just days.

And later as the clouds collect,
And sharp wind whips the grasses,
An officer surveys the scene
Through his fine, brassbound field glasses.

The horses prance and prick their ears,
There's a sudden flight of crows,
And soldiers mutter in the ranks,
As anticipation grows.

Then comes the whine and crump of shot,
As flying spheres of lead
Cut through the lines of marching men,
One ball claims twenty dead.

They break their ranks and scatter,
Some slither in the mud,
As each cannon ball like a meteorite
Lands with a sickening thud

The observer sees most everything
Under that cobalt sky,
And the image most indelible
Is the ease with which men die.

*leopard

The observer's seen it all before,
Unfolding before his gaze,
But he never asks why he created it
In simply seven days.

11

AFTER INKERMAN

No glitter now of sabres,
No fluttering of lace,
No fur or plume or blaze of gold,
Just death's cold, staring face.

Smoke cloaks and chokes and now provokes
A spreading poisonous cloud
That blackens soldiers' faces,
Hangs o'er them like a shroud.

But a triumph has been won here,
A proud feat of British arms,
Each inch of ground most dearly bought,
From the trumpet's first alarms.

Where face to face and blade to blade,
Men bludgeoned, slashed and sabred,
And sweating gunners at their guns,
Died bravely as they laboured.

Already history has been made,
Great acts of dash and daring,
By soldiers from both sides today,
Though death, at men, was staring.

The drums and pipes are silent now,
No trumpets and no bells,
The atmosphere's no longer pierced
By the savage 'Minden Yells'.

Or the famous cry 'Die Hard My Men',
Echoes from long ago,
Reminding every soldier,
He will reap what he will sow.

Shell Hill and Sandbag Battery
Are monuments to the brave,
To those who lived to tell the tale
And those now in the grave.

Inkerman was a soldier's fight,
A tribute to plain men,
Those lion-hearted warriors,
ALL OF WHOM 'WOULD GO AGAIN'.

12

A MOST COURAGEOUS OFFICER

Father, were you at Inkerman
The famous soldiers' battle,
Where plain men fought against the odds
And many heard death's rattle?

Father, were you at Inkerman
On the ridge they call Shell Hill,
Where young men faced down Russian guns,
Do you recall it still?

Father, were you at Inkerman
On that mist enshrouded slope,
Where men were armed – not just with guns,
But courage, faith and hope?

Father, were you at Inkerman,
Did you see the bayonets gleam,
Did you smell the stench of powder,
Did you hear the horses scream?

Father, were you at Inkerman?
Please tell me once again,
I want to hear the story
Of that triumph, joy and pain.

Father, were you at Inkerman,
At the barrier close by the Hill?
Did you see Lieutenant Acton,
Do you recall it still?

Father, were you at Inkerman
When Acton performed his great deed,
When told to attack the Battery
Up that slope through the scrub and at speed?

Father, were you at Inkerman
When that stupendous lesson was taught,
When the bone-weary soldiers, exhausted and wet
At first wouldn't give him support?

Father, were you at Inkerman
When Acton drew his sword from its sheath?
Were you there as he started uphill – on his own
While smoke swirled above like a wreath?

Father, were you at Inkerman
When Acton's action was seen
As a lesson in leadership, courage and skill
On the mist-shrouded slopes of Shell Hill?

Father, were you at Inkerman
When a soldier rose up from the ranks
And cried out with pride, 'Sir I'll stand by your side',
Others followed from left and right flanks?

Father were you at Inkerman
On that glorious day in November
When Acton of the Seventy-Seventh*
Led a charge that we all now remember?

Father, were you at Inkerman
On the ridge they call Shell Hill,
Does memory fade, like an unpolished blade
Or do you remember it still?

Father, you *were* at Inkerman
On the ridge they call Shell Hill.
And I see your face and hear you sigh
And I know you are up there still.

* The 77th Foot (East Middlesex Regiment) formed in 1787, brother
Regiment to the famous 57th (West Middlesex), 'The Diehards'.

13

A GALLANT FOOL
LEWIS EDWARD NOLAN

Down from those rock-strewn rugged heights,
Past gully, shale and boulder,
Into the valley deep below
With no glance o'er his shoulder.

For Captain Nolan of The Light
Was a cavalryman supreme,
And to see The Light Brigade attack,
Was to him a cherished dream.

For he had seen the 'Heavies' charge,
While he'd sat unencumbered,
'Twas gall and wormwood to his soul,
Even though his hour was numbered.

Impatient, headstrong, vital, brave,
A maverick hot for battle,
As against his horse's sweating flanks,
His leather scabbard rattled.

His Irish and Italian blood
Was a pyrotechnic mixture,
Thus to gallop with The Light Brigade
Was in his brain – a fixture.

No thought save one, as he sped down,
Driving his steed yet faster,
He must deliver old Lord Raglan's note,
Not to do so spelled disaster.

Thus sliding, snorting, short of breath,
His horse then reached the valley.
He spurred it on without a pause,
The cavalry he must rally.

An avenging angel from the heights,
Bent on some sacred mission,
He reined his horse at Lord Lucan's front,
By the Heavy Brigade's position.

The note from Lord Raglan is offered out,
While his horse foams and champs at the bit,
For the animal's quite overheated,
And it's hard now for Nolan to sit.

He moves the beast round in a circle,
It's excited and starting to rear,
And Nolan himself in a frenzy,
Is anxious to make himself clear.

'There are your guns sir,' screams Nolan,
Where he points though is still far from clear,
For his horse is constantly moving,
Facing sideways, then front and then rear.

What happens next is just history,
As an order is passed down the line,
To Lord Cardigan seated on 'Ronald',
The charger he rode at the time.

So the Light Brigade trot into legend,
Through cannon smoke, gunshot and flame,
And for years to come men will still wonder,
Is it one man – or three they can blame?

Alas for poor Nolan this question
Is one where there's no way to rule,
For he died in the charge with his comrades.
Was he hero or villain or fool?

14

CARDIGAN
(The Homicidal Earl)

Advancing with style and precision,
Lord Cardigan alone at their head,
A brilliant and most gallant figure
With the heart of a lion 'twas said.

Mounted tall on Ronald his charger,
His uniform bright in the sun,
With gold-laced pelisse on his shoulder,
He trots to the sound of the gun.

His back is as straight as a ramrod,
His gaze is fixed firmly ahead,
And the sword in his hand is quite steady,
This is how the Eleventh are led.

He knows that the charge undertaken,
Is a foolhardy, madcap affair,
And flies in the face of all logic
As the enemy guns roar and flare.

But Cardigan is not one to waver,
Though he rides to the entrance of hell.
He'll not flinch for an inch or just quaver,
Responding to duty's mute bell.

For this is his moment of glory,
The pinnacle of his career,
The obstinate, arrogant soldier
Who holds valour so precious and dear.

All his life has been lived at the gallop,
Drenched in privilege, riches and sport,
A law to himself beyond censure,
Like a Sultan in some Eastern court.

A golden boy pampered from childhood,
With six sisters who worshipped him too,
When those sapphire eyes flashed, all resistance was dashed,
Each indulgence and wish was made true.

A horseman of finest distinction,
And a swordsman of greater repute,
Each tall tree and tower was a challenge,
No gun made that he couldn't shoot.

He grew to be reckless and headstrong,
High tempered and given to rage,
Tall, handsome, precocious and fiery,
A gallant young blade of his age.

But in spite of his physical splendour,
He was volatile, selfish and crass,
And his intellect sadly, was judged very badly,
And there were greybeards who called him an ass.

But as he grew swiftly to manhood,
A Greek god with nothing to fear,
His desire to take arms as a soldier,
Became painfully, obviously clear.

Thus he purchased an early commission,
And was eager and keen to command,
He fancied his role as a leader
With ambitions predictably grand.

As the Colonel to head the Eleventh,
He determined to establish his mark,
Choosing fabulous clothes for his soldiers
And making them drill in Hyde Park.

But he treated subordinates badly,
Was a bully, a braggart, a cheat.
Men were flogged for some mild indiscretion,
Punished sharply unless always neat.

With his tantrums and rages increasing,
If just crossed in the mildest degree,
His behaviour was noted, his insults oft quoted
In the press for the public to see.

Court martials and law suits abounded,
His reputation was roundly condemned,
As he strutted his stuff, no rebuke was enough,
To make certain his ways he'd amend.

Each anger-fuelled antic, drove the Horse Guards quite frantic,
And Lord Hill* was obliged to respond,
He wrote a short letter; 'You must behave better,
As the pale you have now gone beyond.'

But Cardigan, haughty, imperious, naughty,
Shrugged off critics and comrades like flies,
He was Caesar and Czar, a glittering star,
No man living could cut him to size.

Even The Duke**, with a most mild rebuke,
Fell short of demanding his head,
Victoria too, took a liberal view,
Though Albert*** was shocked, it was said.

Thus the Regiment's fame grew bright like a flame,
With Cardigan soaking up glory.
The Eleventh Hussars became peacocks and stars,
Though 'twas far from the end of the story.

* Lord Hill, Army Commander
** The Duke of Wellington
*** Prince Albert, Queen Victoria's husband

When war with the Russians seemed certain,
And British ships sailed from our coast,
The Eleventh were mounted, each bright sabre counted,
'Twas destiny calling, they'd boast.

'Twas soon starkly clear, on the plains of Crimea,
That the war would cut deep to their core,
Though uniforms glittered, men soon were embittered,
And endured deprivations galore.

The story's well known of what happened,
On that fateful day high on the plains,
When the order to charge was first issued
And Cardigan loosened his reins.

That he was a swine and a bounder,
A martinet stiff-necked and loud,
Should not prevent history recording,
He was brave too, though stupid and proud.

15

THE RUSSIAN GUNNER

He kneels beside an iron gun,
Thick bearded like a lion.
If God decrees his life must end,
This is the spot he'll die on.

Below the sloping, tufted hill,
Lies the valley and the plain,
Far distant in the hazy light,
Still glistening from the rain.

Is that a puff of smoke he sees,
Or just a cloud of dust?
It's cavalry, as small as toys,
If his keen eyes he can trust.

They're moving up the valley now,
At a steady walking pace,
He sees brass and silver glittering,
And a fluttering of lace.

Surely now they must manoeuvre
And deploy their serried ranks,
Move at once like well-drilled soldiers,
To one or other of their flanks.

But there's still no sign of wavering
In this progress most serene.
The Russian gunner strokes his beard now
At this unexpected scene.

He can't believe the line will hold
With cannons straight ahead,
And guns in ranks on both their flanks,
Those fools are good as dead.

But now he sees the line move fast
At a steady, jogging trot,
And the gunner takes his ramrod
To prepare his cannon shot.

His sergeant's standing just above him,
With a gloved hand raised up high,
The orders given, 'fire at will' now
And the gunner breathes a sigh.

A deafening roar, a tongue of flame
And clouds of billowing smoke.
The guns recoil and gouge the turf,
Men blink and cough and choke.

The screaming 'whoosh' of cannon balls,
The loud 'crump' as they land,
They bounce along like dervishes
Through turf, soil, rock and sand.

The gunners have their range now,
And the gun drills slick and fast.
The spongeing, loading, ramming, firing
Is followed by the blast.

Through veils of smoke and showers of earth,
From his hilltop battle station,
The gunner sees how cannon fire,
Wreaks death and devastation.

Now the awful scene's unfolding,
Headless corpses riding by,
Upright in their bloody saddles,
Other mounts collapse and die.

Shattered limbs and smoking bodies
Trampled as the charge gets faster,
As they close the gaps between them,
Plunging onward to disaster.

No man wavers, no man pauses,
Onward, onward still they come,
Sabres flashing, horses screaming,
Closing on each Russian gun.

Then the pounding, sweating horses,
Reach the apex of the hill.
Soldiers hack and cut the gunners,
Both sides now intent to kill.

In the smoke and mad confusion,
Sabres clanging like a bell,
Brave men die and fall as heroes,
Peace at last, and free from hell.

The gunner slumps beside his cannon,
Savaged by three sabre cuts,
Next to him an English charger,
Neighing as it spills its guts.

All around him men are fighting,
The air is thick with acrid smoke,
To his left an English soldier,
Tunic ragged, like a cloak.

The gunner feels his life is ebbing,
Lancing pain with every breath,
So he prays for Holy Russia,
Knows that soon he'll meet his death.

Then up close, a strange encounter,
Strong hands help him to his feet,
He's staring at the English soldier,
So close now that he feels his heat.

Then the Englishman collapses
With a little choking cry,
And the gunner kneels beside him,
Waiting for the man to die.

Both the men are scarcely twenty,
Virgins in the art of war.
It's for both, their first encounter,
And for both, there'll be no more.

Lying on the broken hillside,
Side-by-side like stricken sheep,
Life blood oozing from their bodies,
Claimed at last by death's cold sleep.

Heroes both, uncomprehending,
Both convinced their cause was right,
Sent to fight old statesmen's quarrels,
Now they face eternal night.

16

MIGHTIER THAN THE SWORD

William Howard Russell of *The Times*

A scribbler, a reptile, a mercenary hack,
Or merely observer and sage?
Just who was this fellow with notepad and pen
For whom editors held the front page.

He was up at the front in fine fettle,
So close he smelled powder and shot,
On a small canvas chair, with his long poet's hair,
He was there when the fighting grew hot.

His reports to *The Times* were a legend,
Reaching readers in city and shire,
His conclusions were often dramatic,
Word pictures of bloodshed and fire.

Politicians and soldiers in London,
Were eager to read his reports,
Transmitted by cable from Russia,
From ramparts and trenches and forts.

The speed of transmission was awesome,
Shaping public opinion at home,
Causing liberals to choke on their coffee,
And elderly statesmen to groan.

And his critics offered varied opinions,
Of Russell and all of his work,
Some thought him a cad and a bounder,
No more than a newspaper clerk.

But William Howard Russell, in the midst of all this bustle,
Sent his images of conflict straight back home,
And to give the man his due, it was just a personal view,
Impressions, stark and real – and his alone.

His words would sometimes trespass on old men as they ate
    breakfast,
And they often swallowed more than what they ate,
There were photographs as well, showing images of hell,
More than plenty to be piled on any plate.

War reporting then had only just begun,
As future wars were followed like the drum,
One can hazard but a guess, that from every bloody mess,
Truth and victory, both together, could be won.

17

THE ENGLISH CHARGER

With manes flying, nostrils flaring,
Each hoof but a speeding blur,
Flanks gleaming, sweat streaming,
The jingle of harness and spur.

Prancing, dancing, boldly advancing,
At canter, gallop or trot,
Over snow-kissed Russian wastelands,
Or harsh desert, furnace hot.

Stepping nimbly between boulders,
Scrambling at the river's edge,
Skirting craters made by cannon,
Leaping high o'er ditch and hedge.

Some cut low with ball and grapeshot,
Glossy coats smeared wet with blood,
Gaping wounds in chest and withers,
Falling, flailing in the mud.

Long tail flicking, soft ears pricking,
Cool breeze stirring flowing mane,
The noblest beast in all creation
Sharing soldiers' joy and pain.

Our toast then is the English Charger,
Standing tall upon the hill,
Silhouetted by the skyline,
Head held high, his body still.

Immortalised in countless statues,
Carved in marble, bronze and lead,
Replicating bone and muscle,
A work of art, alive or dead.

Although frequently referred to as English Chargers, many of the horses used by the British Cavalry during the Crimean War were from Ireland, and the re-mounts necessary after death from disease or battle were obtained locally. All the mounts which took part in the Charge of the Light Brigade were killed or had to be destroyed, whereas fewer than half the gallant six hundred cavalrymen were casualties.

18

SHAKESPEARE'S TIDE

There's more than one tide in the affairs of men
To be taken at the flood,
And oft the moment that arrives
Is veiled by smoke and blood.

Thus shrouded in confusion,
Deafened by sounds of war,
The opportunity vanishes,
Perhaps 'twill come no more.

But sure as cock crow heralds dawn,
And darkness turns to light,
The tide that Shakespeare spoke of
Floods back with all its might.

Young soldiers fresh to the battle,
See how life there is brutal and cheap,
How the angel of mercy has suddenly left,
Replaced by death's scythe that must reap.

And yet in all battles, there's always a pause,
A moment of silence and peace,
When bone-weary soldiers lay down their guns,
When the killing and dying must cease.

When through clouds of billowing gun smoke,
And across the churned earth of the field,
Men gaze in the eyes of their enemies,
Knowing one or the other must yield.

They rise up from the trench and the rampart,
Move forward with soft measured tread,
To meet face to face and with chivalrous grace,
Shake the hands of men soon to be dead.

19

THE THIN RED LINE

Of all the tales that stir the blood,
And fill good hearts with pride,
There's one that rouses spirits high,
Its thrill has never died.

How often have we heard it told,
With passion, even relish,
A legendry feat of arms,
A memory to cherish?

Out on the bruised and broken plain,
Where warriors collided,
And distant trumpets sounded 'charge',
And men's fate was decided.

Right here upon this very ground,
Now sprung with gorse and heather,
Where ancient rocks are lichen hung,
Kissed smooth by centuries' weather.

A narrow gorge defines this spot
Where British soldiers halt,
This road to Balaklava where
A great battle will be fought.

Above, beyond those verdant hills
That fence the northern valley,
A mighty mass of Russians move,
Each man now set to rally.

With cavalry and heavy guns
Amassed along their flanks,
Spread wide, a savage human tide,
Four thousand in their ranks.

While standing steadfast by the gorge,
Spread on the sloping hill,
A mere five hundred British troops
Face front, alert but still.

These are the gallant Ninety-Third,
Red-coated Highland men,
The cream of Scotland's warriors,
Each man can fight like ten.

Then comes a massive cannonade,
And a fusillade of shot,
As Russian guns belch fire and smoke,
And their barrels grow red hot.

The Highland troops in two ranks deep,
Are ordered to lie still,
As cannon balls come crashing down,
Upon that fateful hill.

'Remember men,' their General cries,
'There will be no retreat,
We cannot let the Russians through,
To do so spells defeat.'

The man who gave these orders,
And earned his glorious fame,
Was a battle-hardened soldier.
Colin Campbell was his name.

Sir Colin was a veteran,
Who bore the scars of war.
He'd fought both under Wellington,
And that hero, Sir John Moore.

In India and in China,
The West Indies and in Spain,
Yet Campbell was no aristocrat,
But a Scotsman dour and plain.

His father was a carpenter,
And his schooling had been short.
Thus his wisdom, skill and enterprise,
Was virtually self-taught.

But now the Russian hordes are close,
Like a lurking tidal wave,
And he will face this motley throng,
Resourceful, strong and brave.

Over the soaring Causeway Heights,
Unseen like wraiths they pour,
Four squadrons strong, a line of steel
To prosecute the war.

Then as these Russian horsemen
Come plunging down the hill,
Five hundred Scots in lines two deep
Stand up, as if at drill.

Amazed, confused and hesitant,
The Russians are checked and halted,
While the Thin Red Line of gallant Scots
Await to be assaulted.

No man flinches, no man wavers,
No Redcoat glances rear,
Each soldier knows if his life's to end,
He's going to sell it dear.

And thus they stand, implacable,
To face the Russian hordes,
The Thin Red Line of Highlanders,
Hearts strong as British swords.

The Russian horsemen waver now,
Rein back their sweating mounts,
As British muskets flare and roar,
And every bullet counts.

The Russians wheel as if to leave,
And the Scots release a cheer.
Some men advance with eagerness,
They show no trace of fear.

But Campbell, ever vigilant,
Calls sternly down the line,
'Damn all this eagerness,' he cries,
'Hold steady, we'll be fine.'

And so they are, these gallant Scots,
Magnificently fine,
With Balaklava saved by those
Who formed the Thin Red Line.

20

THE GALLANT GRENADIER

The Hon. Henry Hugh Manvers Percy
The Heights of Inkerman, 5 November 1854

A grey mist cloaks those rugged heights
With a cloying, damp embrace,
It masks ravines and gullies
And obscures each soldier's face.

The broken ground is treacherous,
Sewn coarse with tufted grass,
And thickets ribbed with dragon's teeth
Over which each man must pass.

On that bleak November morning,
The Russian hordes advance
Towards the Sandbag Battery,
For 'tis here they see their chance.

They've poured forth from Sevastopol,
And seek to drive a wedge
Between the French and British troops,
Then occupy the ledge.

A pincer movement is the plan,
And the Russian generals' boast,
To isolate the British on the hill,
Cut all routes to the coast.

The British front line takes the shock
Of the surge of Russian troops,
As they stream in thousands up the slopes
Now emitting fiercesome whoops.

Still early in the morning,
For dawn has scarcely broken,
And reinforcements to these British troops
Is now a need unspoken.

Down on the plain below the Heights,
The Brigade of Guards is waking,
Each man responding to the bugle call,
All heroes in the making.

Still groggy from sleep's warm embrace,
That nocturnal paradise,
They snap alert at their sergeant's cry,
Battle-ready in a trice.

No breakfast now, no warming cup,
No time to wash or shave,
No lingering over what lies ahead,
Be it glory or the grave.

The Russians swarm like insects
Onto that fateful hill,
Past sandbags and embrasures,
Each man intent to kill.

Grenadiers are there to face them,
With bayonets and swords,
A steady line of Englishmen
'Gainst howling Russian hordes.

The fighting is ferocious,
Men stab and cut and hack,
The enemy is repulsed, and yet –
Those Tartars have come back!

Six times or more – no man keeps score,
The Sandbag Battery's taken,
Then lost again midst murderous toil,
Each charge faced down and shaken.

The Russians mass and charge again
As they scramble up the slopes,
And for a moment – scarcely more,
They raise up Russian hopes.

The Grenadiers are fading fast,
Their casualties horrific,
They need to rally desperately,
With energy prolific.

Each weary soldier racked with pain,
Lungs burning fit to burst,
And sweat or blood on every brow,
On every lip a curse.

And just ahead, upon the hill,
A heaving, human tide,
A living, breathing testament
To vaulting Russian pride.

The British troops observe this scene,
The hill is thick with Russians.
Can they be driven off again
Without fatal repercussions?

But then among those weary men,
The wounded and the dead,
Henry Percy holds his sword aloft
And moves up to their head.

'Now come on boys,' is his trenchant call,
'Our duty is quite plain,
We must attack, we must go back
And take that hill again.'

Then into that press of human flesh,
Now swarming on the hill,
Young Percy plunges, as Russian lunges,
Surround him for the kill.

He sees the Russian musketeers,
Fire downhill at his men,
But he finds this 'quite impertinent'
As he scales the slope again.

Breathless he climbs the parapet,
Exchanging cuts and blows,
When a chunk of stone is hurled at him,
Smashing hard into his nose.

The fight around him rages on,
With the British in full cry,
As Percy regains consciousness,
Though he's half blind in one eye.

A subaltern revives him
With brandy from his flask,
And Percy's on his feet again,
Keen to complete his task.

But now the tide is turning,
How strange the twists of fate,
For the enemy's retreating fast,
At a tumbling, stumbling gait.

Although his sight is clouded,
Henry Percy too has seen
The Russians fanning down the hill
To St Clement's great ravine.

He charges now in hot pursuit,
With ninety of his men,
And other troops upon the hill,
Are keen to go again.

Yet just beyond the deep ravine,
Lies a mass of Russian steel,
Packed ranks of gleaming bayonets,
British flesh is soon to feel.

But Percy sees the danger there,
At the gaping mouth of hell,
His gallant lads face certain death
If they tumble down pell-mell.

Half-blinded and face blackened,
Dead soldiers at his feet,
His orders are to 'stand fast',
No advance and no retreat.

'Keep firing lads,' is Percy's cry,
'Til every round is spent,'
But all about the Russians swarm,
Each man on victory bent.

Ammunition is in short supply,
Each moment it grows shorter,
They have to disengage at once,
Or they'll face bloody slaughter.

Here skill and field craft and quick wits
Are now deployed by Percy.
He's seen a bank, close by a spur
That might offer, briefly, mercy.

They find a sheep track on their right,
By Inkerman's great knoll,
But fire, alas, from their own troops,
Adds more death to the toll.

And thus, exhausted, wounded,
Henry Percy and his men,
Reach camp at last, depleted,
Having lost a score and ten.

Relief and pride that they've survived,
Is soon replaced by pain,
As those unharmed are soon re-armed,
And sent back to fight again.

The battle flares til four o'clock,
But at last is dearly won,
And many thousand men will die
Before the setting of the sun.

The Grenadiers' own losses
Are prodigious on the day.
Forty-six percent are hurt or killed
In that awesome, bloody fray.

But those who live to tell the tale,
Those spared by God's great mercy,
Remember one fine gallant man,
His name, why Henry Percy.

21

THE RECRUIT

He was a fool and a rogue and a murderer,
With morals both coarsened and loose,
And over his bleak life was looming,
The shadow of gallows and noose.

But he'd take the Sovereign's shilling,
This scurvy and feckless young knave,
Though he cared not a jot for his Sovereign,
And his soul was too blackened to save.

He was drunk as a skunk and he stank like a hound,
And he cursed and hollered and brawled,
He was clamped in the stocks, still riddled with pox,
And all over him slimy things crawled.

Reviled and rebuked as he lay there and puked,
With an effort he raised up his head,
And there past his feet, stood a man tall and neat,
In a shako and tunic of red.

'I'm Sergeant Moran,' cried the stranger,
'And I'm here on behalf of the Queen,
So dispense with this strife, get a new start in life,
See the world with its sights most serene.

'Traverse oceans and deserts exotic,
Learn to handle a musket and blade,
Pluck hot kisses from ladies erotic,
And for all this my lad – you'll get paid.

'So become a recruit, learn to march, drill and shoot,
Wear a uniform cut to perfection,
If you're eager and willing to take the Queen's shilling,
Of young women you'll have your selection.'

The sergeant then offered him porter,
And a half-dozen puffs on his pipe,
The fellow was rank – dear God how he stank,
And the stench of his sweat was now ripe.

And thus he was fully persuaded,
To follow the sound of the drum,
Released from the stocks in an instant,
Back blistered and raw from the sun.

'Now just follow me lad, to the barracks,'
Said the sergeant re-lighting his pipe,
'I'm sure you'll be pleased when you get there,
The Queen's army needs more of your type.'

After walking ten leagues from the village,
They arrived at the old army camp,
By a gate made of roughly hewn timber,
And lit by a huge swinging lamp.

They passed tethered horses that snorted and stamped,
And cannons of iron and brass,
And tall canvas tents topped with fluttering flags,
Pitched in rows by the coarse meadow grass.

To the wide barrack square topped with cinder,
Where before them in six ragged rows,
Were assembled a group of young peasants,
Dressed in shabby farm labourers' clothes.

They were marched to the edge of the barracks,
A bewildered and shuffling throng,
Where two corporals were waiting with buckets,
Each handle a stout leather thong.

All were made to strip naked as jay birds,
Thin bodies exposed to the sun,
And the corporals up-ended the buckets,
Sluicing down each recruit one-by-one.

'Tonight you all sleep under canvas,'
Cried Sergeant Moran to the men,
'And tomorrow you'll all begin training,
You'll get boots and a uniform – then –

'You'll pick up a musket and maybe a sword,
And you'll learn to march proudly with dash,
And now that you're soldiers of our Sovereign Queen,
If you're idle you'll soon taste the lash.

'We'll beat you in shape if we have to,
But in six weeks or probably less,
You'll be ready to fight for your country,
Walk tall – and be a success.'

Society's dregs and pariahs,
Once described as the scum of the earth,
But marching behind flying colours,
They'll be heroes and soldiers of worth.

For soon they'll have comrades and friendship,
And a sense of belonging at last,
As gallant young blades of old England,
In this honourable role they'll be cast.

They'll learn how to kill with a sabre,
How to stand under fire side by side,
How to endure pain, withstand frost, snow and rain,
But above all they'll learn to feel pride.

And gentlemen of England, now abed,
Should rise and raise a glass,
To toast these saucy hooligans,
As the Empire's warrior class.

22

BEGGARS ON HORSEBACK

After the Siege of Sevastopol, British soldiers received back pay of up to three shillings a day. This they spent largely on alcohol and became roaring drunk. Captain Hopton Bassett Scott of the 9th was horrified and in a letter home, described the inebriated soldiers as 'Beggars on Horseback'. 'Put a beggar on horseback,' he wrote, 'and see how he will ride – nothing will suit our privates now, but champagne!'

Decanted from those mighty ships
In eighteen fifty four,
And landed on the coastline
Of a rugged, wind-tossed shore.

Each soldier peacock-pristine,
Each shako shiny black,
With gorgeous scarlet tunics
On every man-jack's back.

But scarce a month would come to pass,
With wind and foulest weather,
When vivid scarlet soon would fade
And cracks appear in leather.

The mud, the rain, the blazing sun,
In searing equal parts,
While failing to down spirits,
Or diminish English hearts –

– Played havoc with appearances,
Each man a ragged scruff;
Unwashed, be-grimed and lousy,
Like a footpad or a rough.

But even worse, 'tis sad to say,
Is what Lord Raglan feared,
As men cast down their razors
And on each chin grew a beard.

This was a 'foreign fancy',
A habit of the French,
And soon a pack of 'monkeys'
Peeped out from every trench.

This was alas a prelude
In those fields of the Crimea,
As soldiers received 'back pay',
And spent it all on beer.

So stinking, drinking, roistering,
Was the order of the day,
And even junior officers
Now chose to 'look away'.

Excesses quite exceptional,
Spread swiftly through the ranks,
Those officers who tried to help
Received abuse – not thanks.

But those who wallowed in their cups,
Had been through grape and shell,
Faced musket balls and cannon blasts,
A blood-soaked fiery hell.

Yes, all of them in that motley crew,
Down to the humblest man,
Had stormed the massive ramparts
Of the precipitous Redan.

So history perhaps
Will tell a kinder story,
Of courage, fortitude and guts,
Mixed with the blood and glory.

For all those English rascals,
Who fought in this great battle,
All those who lived to tell the tale,
And those who felt death's rattle.

So we salute this hirsute mob,
This rag and tag and bobble,
Though they were drunks, and stank like skunks,
They got England out of trouble.

23

TODLEBEN

What seek to seize Sevastopol,
That glittering Russian prize?
To wreck its mighty ramparts,
Pluck out its heart and eyes?

Not while my heart beats strongly,
Not while my blood runs hot,
Not while the sons of Russia fight
And have fired the last brave shot.

For we have built defences,
Formidable and vast,
As defender of Sevastopol
Is the role in which I'm cast.

For I am Colonel Todleben,
A soldier engineer,
I offer to both God and Czar
My life and my career.

Let English muskets smoke and flare,
French cannons spew forth lead,
For we will fight with Slavic might,
No man will pause til dead.

Come foulest thunder, crack the sky
And lightning blaze and streak,
Let horses, guns and fighting men
On us their terror wreak.

For I am Colonel Todleben,
A prince of engineers,
I've made Sevastopol inviolate
For at least a thousand years.

Lieutenant-Colonel Franz Edouard Ivanovitch Todleben was an engineering genius who masterminded the fortifications of Sevastopol. Had the allies attempted their siege earlier, before Todleben had had time to complete his defences, they might have taken it at the first attempt.

First bombardment of Sevastopol	17 October (1854)
Second bombardment	9 April (1855)
Third bombardment	6 June (1855)
Fourth bombardment	17 June (1855)
Fifth bombardment	17 August (1855)
Final bombardment	5 September (1855)

The allies entered Sevastopol on 9 September (1855)
Treaty of Peace signed in Paris on 30 March (1856)
Treaty ratified in Paris on 27 April (1856)

24

SEVASTOPOL – 27 September

Was the City of Sevastopol
A ripe fruit set to fall?
With few redoubts encircling it
And a loose-built earth park wall?

Was it a prize worth plucking?
Could Russian guns be still?
Would soldiers simply march through
And little blood be spilled?

The French were counselling caution,
But many disagreed,
George Cathcart* of the gallant Fourth
Cried, 'Strike at once with speed!'

Lord Raglan, the Commander,
Was one who first agreed,
But Sir John Burgoyne** was adamant,
'It is siege guns that we need'.

'Let us first blast those defences,
Let them hear our cannons' crack,
We'll reduce those walls to rubble
Before our men attack.'

* Sir George Cathcart, Commander of the Fourth Division who held a
dormant commission to succeed Raglan in the event of his death.
** Sir John Burgoyne, Inspector General of Fortifications.

But Cathcart, just like Nolan*,
Was impatient to proceed,
'Siege guns will take too long,' he said,
'They'll not serve our urgent need.'

'We should attack immediately,
While resistance is still weak,
We must strike now Lord Raglan,
If swift victory you seek.'

The noble Lord thus counselled,
Was torn 'twixt this and that,
'What should I do?' he murmured
As he fiddled with his hat.

The French were firm and resolute
'Gainst action swift and stark,
For their heavy siege artillery
They would need to disembark.

Thus caution 'twas that won the day,
Not dash and bold heroics,
No chance for gallant soldiers now
To shine, but just be stoics.

Was it cowardice or caution,
Or just toadying to the French?
Was the decision less than manly,
More like a dithering wench?

Historians may disagree
And take a hostile line,
But hindsight is a luxury
As you gaze back over time.

* Captain Edward Lewis Nolan, excitable Cavalry Officer who carried
Lord Raglan's fateful note to Lord Lucan and Lord Cardigan before the
Charge of The Light Brigade.

The failure to attack at once
Had one quite clear effect,
The Russians now had breathing space
Defences to erect.

Their mastermind defender,
Who showed no hint of fear,
Was that genius Colonel Todleben,
The Czar's great engineer.

Inspired and led by Todleben,
The Russians set to work.
Ten thousand men, some merely boys,
Not one among them shirked.

Redoubts and walls and ramparts,
Shallow trenches for their guns,
A line of stout defences
To protect their Russian sons.

This was how the legend started,
And today the tale's still told,
How Sevastopol was defended
By heroes fierce and bold.

So who won this mighty battle,
Who planted victory's seed?
This all depends, dear reader,
On which history you read.

25

The Soldiers

Soft breezes stir the grasses,
Zephyrs' breath like a ghostly kiss,
Silent guns with mouths still open,
No more a threat than a serpent's hiss.

Soil engorged with the blood of soldiers,
Replete with bones now white as milk,
Twisted oaks with stunted branches,
Caught in a fork a scrap of silk.

Once a bright and fluttering pennant
Of regiment proud and bold,
Now without its sturdy banner,
Just a memory edged in gold.

Side by side young boon companions
Never parted e'en in death,
Buried shallow on the hillside,
Graves caressed by winter's breath.

These were boys, not ancient adults,
Virgin beards on each soft cheek.
All came here to serve their country,
In praise of them, let history speak.

They were English, French and Russian,
Scots and Turks, yes all the same,
Pawns cast down by venerable statesmen
In that great and awful game.

Years slip by like passing shadows,
To faint echoes of a bugle call.
Is it true that ghosts of soldiers
Centuries on can still walk tall?

Keep the memory clear and vivid,
Of those children of the night,
Salute these simple, splendid soldiers,
Brothers all, who came to fight.